My Amazing Toddler **Behavioral Series**

I Have A BIG Job.
I Am A BIG BROTHER!

An Affirmation-Themed Toddler Book About Getting A Sibling (Ages 2-4)

By Suzanne T. Christian

TWORAVENS
BOOKS

Two Little Ravens
CHILDREN'S NON-FICTION BOOKS

Paperback Edition: 9781964202594
Hardcover Edition: 9781964202600
Digital Edition: 9781964202617

Published in the United States by Two Ravens Books LLC,
254 Chapman Rd, Ste 209, Newark DE 19702

'Expand the mind, free the imagination, one title at a time.'
www.tworavensbooks.com

Welcome to
"I Have A Big Job. I Am A Big Brother!"

This heartfelt book is a toddler-friendly guide that helps your little one embrace the excitement of a new sibling. Within these pages, you'll find easy-to-understand affirmations and relatable scenarios emphasizing empathy, pride, and cooperation.

Vibrant illustrations capture everyday moments, transforming each reading session into a fun, confidence-building experience.

By revisiting these gentle reminders, your child gains a stronger sense of self-worth while learning to nurture their new sibling with kindness and patience.

Prepare for a joyful journey of bonding and discovery as you empower your child to be the best big brother they can be!

Suzanne T. Christian

I am a big brother, and this is my special job!

I love to make funny faces
so Baby _____ will smile.

My gentle hands keep
Baby _____ safe.
I am a big brother!

I can show Baby _____ my favorite toy when Mommy is busy.

Sometimes I feel sad when Mummy cuddles Baby _____, but I know Mummy loves me too!

Even when Mommy
holds Baby
_____,
she still loves me.

I can help change diapers
by handing wipes—
what a big job!

I can show Baby _____ how to clap hands. That's a fun game!

Baby _____'s tiny hands
hold my finger, and it makes me smile.

When Baby _____ cries,
I can bring a soft toy to help.
I am a big brother!

My gentle hugs make Baby _____
feel warm and loved. I am a big brother!

I use my quiet voice when Baby _____ sleeps.

I love reading to
Baby _____.
Sometimes the words
are silly!

I have a big job. I can help get Baby _____'s bottle. I am a big brother!

It's fun to make Baby _____ laugh with a silly peekaboo.

I can teach Baby ＿＿＿＿＿
how to roll a ball.

roll, roll, roll!

If Baby _____ is noisy,
I stay nice and calm.

It's okay if Baby _____ cries a lot—
That's how babies talk!

I can help Baby
learn new words:
"Mama," "Dada," and
"Bro!"

I can give Baby _____
a gentle kiss on the head.

When Baby _____ smiles,
I feel so happy!

I Have A Big Job.
I Am A Big
BROTHER!
The End!

My Amazing Toddler Behavioral Series

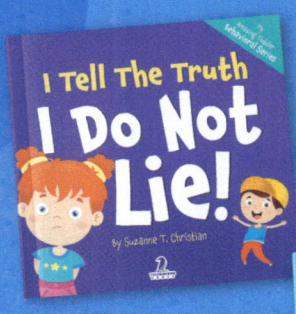

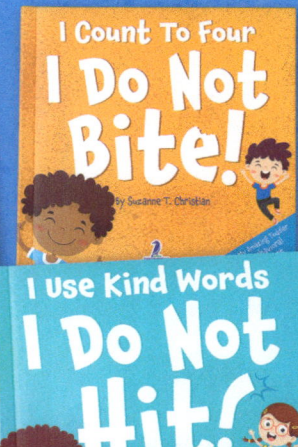

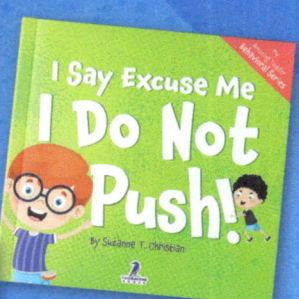

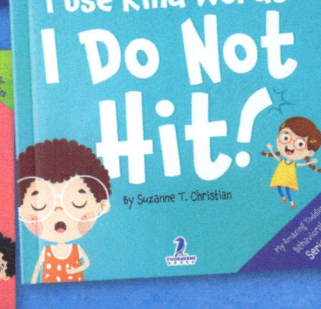

Check Out
Suzanne T. Christian's beloved series
'My Amazing Toddler Behavioral Series'.
Young readers are sure to enjoy!

Two Little Ravens
CHILDREN'S NON-FICTION BOOKS

Dear Amazing Reader,

Thank you for diving into **I Have A Big Job. I Am A Big Brother!** with me. If this book touched your heart or made a difference for a young reader, I'd be grateful if you could share your thoughts in a review. Your feedback inspires my future work and helps others discover the magic within these pages.

I'd love to hear from you directly if you have suggestions or ideas for improving the book. Please feel free to reach out to me at **suzanne.christian@tworavensbooks.com.** Your voice counts, and I cherish it deeply.

With heartfelt gratitude,

www.ingramcontent.com/pod-product-compliance
Lightning Source LLC
Chambersburg PA
CBHW041437120626

46547CB00002B/254